i can CRoCheT

Table of Contents

ican CROCHET

Things You Need to Know

Crochet is more than a hobby. It is an art form that has survived for thousands of years. Crochet has even been found in the tombs of ancient kings and queens.

With crochet, you can express your own style.

You can create things for yourself as well as gifts for all your family and friends.

Crochet also helps to develop hand and eye coordination and stimulates both the creative and logical thought processes in the brain.

STUFF YOU NEED

Only a few things are needed to crochet, like yarn, a hook and a needle. Some you may need to buy and some you may already have at home.

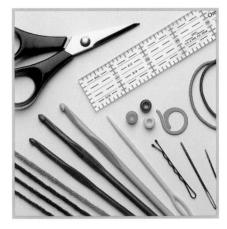

PATTERN SUPPLIES

Each pattern has a list of supplies and special tools needed to make the project, like how much of each color yarn you need and what size hook to use.

CROCHET HOOKS

Crochet hooks come in a wide range of sizes. The sizes are marked on the hook as a letter or a number (see photo 1). The best size to start with is a G hook. You will be using a G hook, an H hook and an I hook for the patterns in this book.

YARN

There are many types of yarn and they come in a special, loosely wrapped ball called a skein. You will be using worsted yarn for all of the projects in this book.

Some skeins are specially made so you do not have to rewind them into a ball like old-fashioned skeins.

First, take the outside strand (see photo 2) and pull it out of the end it is tucked into. This end keeps the skein from coming loose until you are ready to use it. Now the center strand will come out easily.

A large tapestry needle is used for sewing crochet pieces together. This kind of needle has a large eye

so thick yarn will fit through it.

Skein wrappers have extra information about the yarn, such as the amount, color name, dye lot number, care and washing instructions.

When you are picking the colors of yarn for your project, make sure all of the dye lot numbers written on the yarn label are the same *(see photo 3)*.

ART. E300   **Dye lot number**

COLOR: 959 Gemstone

DYE LOT 2   05   7028

Please purchase sufficient yarn of the same dye lot number to complete your project.

S.V.P. acheter suffisamment de fil d'un même bain de teinture pour garder l'uniformité de la teinte.

Por favor compre suficiente el hilo del mis para asegurar uniformidad en el color.

3

There are needle threaders to help get the yarn through the eye of the needle. First, fit the curve at the end of the threader through the eye, then put the end of the yarn in the curve, and finally pull the yarn back through the eye with the threader *(see photo 4)*.

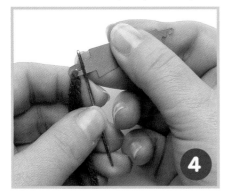

4

If you don't have a needle threader, fold a narrow strip of paper over the end of the yarn and push the paper through the eye.

You will need a pair of scissors to cut the yarn when you are finished.

Crochet patterns usually do not list things like scissors and needle threaders in the materials list. It is understood that you will always need them. ●

Now you are ready to crochet!

i can CROCHET

Lesson 1
Getting Started

WHAT IS CROCHET?

Basically, crochet is making fabric with yarn by pulling one loop through another loop with a hook.

TO BEGIN

A slip knot is the first thing you make in every crochet project. It attaches the yarn to the hook and makes your first loop.

Most patterns will not tell you to make a slip knot because it is done every time you start.

To Make a Slip Knot:

Step 1. Make a loop in the yarn *(see photo 1)*.

Step 2. Reach through the loop, pick up the strand *(see photo 1)*; holding both ends of the yarn, pull the strand through the loop *(see photo 2)*.

You now have a slip knot *(see photo 3)*.

Step 3. Put the loop on the hook and pull the short end of the yarn just a little to tighten the knot *(see photo 4)*.

If you pull too much, the slip knot will be too tight and it will be hard to adjust the size of the loop.

You can tell if the knot is tied right by pulling on the ends. When you pull the short end, the loop should get larger. When you pull the long end, the loop should get smaller.

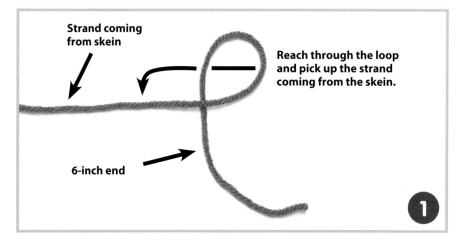

Strand coming from skein

Reach through the loop and pick up the strand coming from the skein.

6-inch end

1

2

3

Slip knot

4

You want the loop to be large enough so the end of the hook will go through it easily without getting caught.

Practice tying a slip knot before moving on to the next step.

There are several ways to hold the yarn and hook. Try each one and choose the way that feels the best to you.

To Hold the Hook & Yarn

Step 1. Hold the hook in one hand like a pencil *(see photo 5)* or like a knife *(see photo 6)*.

Section of strand you will use on the hook

Step 2. Put the yarn in your other hand like you see it in photo 7 and pinch the slip knot with your middle finger and thumb like you see it in photo 8. This keeps the loop on the hook from spinning and sliding around while you crochet.

Practice holding the hook and yarn until it feels comfortable in your hands. The important thing is to hold the yarn in a way that feels right to you. Just make sure it is wrapped over your index finger and you are able to hold the slip knot between the middle finger and thumb.

The yarn stretched between your index finger and the slip knot is the part you use to make stitches *(see photo 8)*.

How tight you keep the yarn wrapped around the little finger controls how fast the yarn slides through your hand. If it is going faster than you want, you can weave it through several fingers to slow it down. ●

ican CROCHET

Chain Stitch Necklace

In this pattern, you will learn to make a chain (ch) stitch. You will also learn to fasten off.

Materials
- Medium (worsted) weight yarn: small amount color of choice
- Size I/9/5.5mm crochet hook
- Tapestry needle

Necklace

STRAND
Make 3 (this means to make 3 Strands)
Make chains until your Strand is 30 inches long or the length you want.

To Make a Chain Stitch
Step 1. Make a slip knot and put it on the hook.

Step 2. Wrap the yarn over the hook from **back to front** *(see photo 1)*. This is called a *yarn over* (yo). This is what you do when you see the letters "yo" in a crochet pattern.

Wrap yarn over front of hook.

1

Step 3. Twist the hook so the front is facing down and pull the hook to the right so the yarn over goes through the loop on the hook and the loop on the hook slides off.

The first chain is done and a new loop is on the hook *(see photo 2)*.

For each chain, yarn over and pull it through the loop on the hook.

Remember to pinch the chain just below the hook every few stitches to keep them below the hook *(see photo 3)*. If you let go of the chain, you will lose control and the loop will spin and slide around on the hook.

Continue making chains. When your strand is long enough, you are ready to cut and hide the yarn end. This is called fastening off.

To Fasten Off

Step 1. Cut the yarn about 6 inches past the loop on the hook. Yarn over with the 6-inch end and pull the end all the way through the loop *(see illustration 1)*.

Illustration 1

Step 2. To hide the end of the yarn, thread it through the tapestry needle and weave the thread through the back of the stitches *(see illustration 2)*.

Illustration 2

Finishing

Hold all 3 Strands together as one, tie knot at one end. Now tie knot in other end.

You may make more or less Strands to make your Necklace bigger or smaller. ●

t!p

When you see the letters "ch" in a crochet pattern, you make a chain stitch. Sometimes there will be a number in front of these letters. This number tells you how many chains to make.

ican CROCHET

Lesson 3
Single Crochet Scrunchie

In this pattern, you will learn how to make a single crochet (sc) stitch worked around a ring. You will also be making a chain (ch) stitch from Lesson 2.

MATERIALS
- Medium (worsted) weight yarn:
    1 oz/50 yds/28g color of choice
- Size G/6/4mm crochet hook
- Elastic ponytail band

Scrunchie
Make a single crochet around the elastic band.

TO MAKE A SINGLE CROCHET AROUND A RING
Step 1. Put a slip knot on the hook and hold it above the ring (see photo 1).

Step 2. Insert the hook through the ring, yarn over (see photo 2) and pull it back through the ring.

You now have 2 loops on the hook (see photo 3).

Step 3. Yarn over again and pull the yarn through both loops on the hook *(see arrow on photo 4)*.

The first single crochet is done and a new loop is on the hook *(see photo 5)*.

Now make 20 chains. For the next single crochet, repeat steps 2 and 3 *(see photo 6)*.

Keep making chain-20 loops and single crochet stitches around the ring until the elastic band is covered.

When you have made all the loops you want for your Scrunchie, you are ready to fasten off *(see Lesson 2 on page 6)*. ●

t!p

When you see the letters "sc" in a crochet pattern, you make a single crochet. Sometimes there will be a number in front of these letters. This tells you how many stitches on the last row or round to work into.

Lesson 4
Half Double Crochet Friendship Bracelet

In this pattern, you will learn to make a regular single crochet (sc) stitch and a half double crochet (hdc) stitch.

You will also be making a chain (ch) stitch from Lesson 2.

Crochet can be decorated with beads and buttons, as well as many other items. They can be added to the yarn and pulled into place as you work, or you can sew them on the finished piece with needle and thread.

Materials
- Medium (worsted) weight yarn:
  1 oz/50 yds/28g
  color of choice
- Size G/6/4mm crochet hook
- Tapestry needle
- Pony beads: 10

Bracelet

Row 1: Thread the yarn on the tapestry needle and string 10 beads onto the yarn *(see photo 1)*.

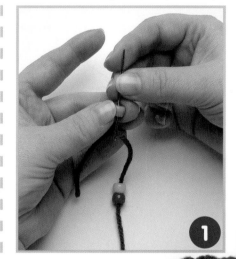

Take the needle off the yarn. These beads will be pushed along the yarn until they are needed in the pattern. Make 28 chains.

This strand of chain stitches is called a starting chain and it is used as the foundation for your first row of stitches.

Make a single crochet in the 2nd chain from the hook *(see photo 2)*.

Second chain from hook

Center of V

Remember not to count the loop on the hook as a chain. For the foundation row only, be sure to go through the center of the V of the chain and under the bump at the back, and do not twist the chain.

Next, make a single crochet in each chain across to the end *(see photo 3)*.

Now you are ready to **turn**. This changes the direction of the first row so you can work the new row from right to left.

To Turn
Flip the row of stitches over so the back of the stitches are facing you *(see photo 4)*.

Row 2: Make 2 chains *(see photo 5)*.

This first strand of chain stitches is called a **turning chain**.

The turning chain is used and counted as a regular stitch unless the instructions tell you not to use it. Always skip the first stitch where the turning chain is worked.

Make a half double crochet in the next stitch on the last row.

To Make a Half Double Crochet

Step 1. Yarn over *(see photo 6)*, and insert the hook through the top two loops of the next stitch *(see photo 7)*.

Step 2. Yarn over again and pull through the stitch *(see photo 8)*; you have 3 loops on the hook.

Step 3. Yarn over and pull through all 3 loops on the hook at the same time.

The first half double crochet is done and a new loop is on the hook *(see photo 9)*.

Make a hdc in the next stitch on the last row.

*Pull a bead on the yarn up next to the stitch just made *(see photo 10)*, make 1 chain,

skip the next stitch on the last row, make a half double crochet in each of the next 2 stitches *(see photo 11)*, repeat from the * 9 more times.

t!p

When you see the letters "hdc" in a crochet pattern, you make a half double crochet. Sometimes there will be a number in front of these letters. This tells you how many stitches on the last row or round to work into.

To Repeat From a * Symbol

Go back to the * and work all of the instructions again until you reach the word "repeat." In this pattern, you will repeat the instructions the number of times after the 2nd * symbol.

After all of the repeats are done, turn.

Row 3: Make 1 chain, make a single crochet in each stitch and in each chain across row 2, **do not turn.**

You will be making the next part in the ends of the rows.

To Work in the End of a Row

As you make a stitch, you insert the hook through loops on the side of the last stitch in the row.

For the **first tie**, thread 1 bead onto yarn, make 1 chain, insert the hook in the end of row 3, yarn over and pull through, [insert the hook in the end of the next row, yarn over and pull through] twice *(see photo 12)*.

When there is a set of parenthesis ( ) symbols or bracket [ ] symbols, you will repeat only the instructions between the symbols.

When there is a number of times after the 2nd bracket symbol, you will repeat the instructions that many times.

You should have 4 loops on the hook, yarn over and pull through all 4 loops *(see photo 13)*, make

14 chains *(see photo 14)*, pull up bead, make 1 chain. Fasten off.

For the **2nd tie**, thread 1 bead onto yarn, make a slip knot and put it on the hook, insert the hook in the other end of row 1, yarn over and pull through, [insert the hook in the end of the next row, yarn over and pull through] twice, yarn over and pull through all 4 loops, make 14 chains, pull up bead, make 1 chain. Fasten off. ●

Lesson 5
Double Crochet Scarf

In this pattern, you will learn to make a double crochet (dc) stitch. You will also be making a chain (ch) stitch from Lesson 2.

You will be working turned rows and you will also learn to make Fringe.

Materials
- Medium (worsted) weight yarn:
  3½ oz/175 yds/100g color of choice
- Size G/6/4mm crochet hook

Scarf

Row 1: Make 23 chains, make a double crochet in the 4th chain from the hook.

To Make a Double Crochet
Step 1. Yarn over and insert the hook in the fourth stitch from the hook *(see photo 1)*. Remember you will never count the loop on the hook as a stitch. For the foundation row only be sure to go through the center of the V of the

stitch and under the bump at the back, and do not twist the chain.

Step 2. Yarn over again and pull through the stitch, you have 3 loops on the hook *(see photo 2)*.

Step 3. Yarn over and pull through 2 loops on the hook *(see photo 3)*.

Step 4. Yarn over again and pull through last 2 loops on the hook.

The first double crochet is done and a new loop is on the hook *(see photo 4)*.

Make a double crochet in each remaining chain of the starting chain, turn counterclockwise.

Row 2: Make 3 chains *(see photo 5)*.

Remember, this strand of chains is called a turning chain and they count the same as a double crochet stitch. You will skip the first double crochet and begin working the first two double crochets below in the second crochet stitch from the hook. Be sure to insert hook under top two loops of stitch.

Make a double crochet in each of the next 2 stitches on the last row, [make 1 chain, skip the next stitch on the last row, make a double crochet in the next stitch] 8 times, make a double crochet in the next stitch, make the last double crochet in the top of the turning chain at the end of row 1 *(see photo 6)*, turn.

Remember, the turning chain is used just like a stitch unless the pattern says to do something else.

Row 3: Make 3 chains, make a double crochet in each of the next 2 stitches on the last row, [make 1 chain, skip the next chain on the last row, make a double crochet in the next stitch *(see photo 7)*] 8 times, make a double crochet in each of the last 2 stitches, turn.

Rows 4–66: Repeat row 3 over and over until you have 66 rows or until Scarf is as long as you want. **Before making it really long**, make sure you have enough extra yarn for the additional length.

Row 67: Make 3 chains, make a double crochet in each stitch and in each chain across to end. Fasten off.

Fringe

Make a 7-inch Fringe in each stitch across each short end of the Scarf.

To Make a Fringe

Step 1. Cut a piece from the skein of yarn 14 inches long. Fold the piece of yarn in half *(see illustration A)*.

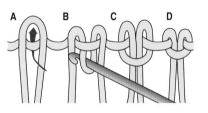

Basic Fringe

Step 2. Insert the hook through a stitch or space, catch the folded end with the hook and pull the folded end of the yarn back through *(see illustration B)*.

Step 3. Insert the hook through the folded end, catch the ends of the yarn with the hook and pull them back through the fold *(see illustration C)*.

Step 4. Pull on the ends to tighten the Fringe in place *(see illustration D)*.

When all of the Fringe are done, trim the ends to make them even. ●

Lesson 6
Slip Stitch Cellphone Bag

In this pattern, you will learn to make a slip stitch (sl st). You will also be making a chain (ch) stitch from Lesson 2, a single crochet (sc) from Lesson 3 and a half double crochet (hdc) stitch from Lesson 5.

You will be working turned rows. You will also learn to join with a single crochet and learn to crochet pieces together.

Materials
- Medium (worsted) weight yarn:
    - 2 oz/100 yds/57g solid color
    - 1 oz/50 yds/28g multicolored yarn
- Size H/8/5mm crochet hook

Bag

SIDE
Make 2.

Row 1: Using the solid color, make 15 chains, make a half double crochet in 2nd chain from hook (see photo 1), make a half double crochet in each chain across, turn.

Row 2: Make 2 chains [this is your turning chain we made in Lesson 4], make a half double crochet in each second chain from hook and in each stitch across, turn.

Rows 3–16: Rep row 2 over and over until you have 16 rows or as many as you need to make this piece about 6 inches long. At end of last row, fasten off.

To Join With a Single Crochet

Step 1. Hold both Side pieces together, matching rows so that row 16 is at top. You will be working through both pieces at same time. Using multicolored yarn, make a slip knot and place the slip knot on hook.

Step 2. Insert hook through both Side pieces at same time (see photo 2), yarn over and pull loop through pieces.

Step 3. Yarn over again and pull loop through both loops on hook (see photo 3).

Evenly space single crochet stitches down 1 long side edge to bottom (see photo 4),

make 3 single crochet in same stitch when you reach the corner stitch, single crochet evenly in chains on opposite side of row 1 across the bottom, make 3 single crochet stitches in the same stitch at the 2nd corner, evenly space single crochet stitches up the remaining side to the last row. **Do not fasten off.** Leave the stitches of last edge open for the top.

Too many stitches worked across the edge will make it ruffle (see photo 5).

Not enough stitches will make it curl up (see photo 6).

SLIP STITCH STRAP

Step 1. Make 35 chain stitches, to connect to end of the Strap, go over to the opposite end of row 16 at top *(see photo 7)*.

Step 2. Make a single crochet in same place as where you worked the join with single crochet *(see photo 8)*. **Do not fasten off**.

To Make a Slip Stitch

Step 1. Turn work so you can work back across the chain stitches on the Strap you just made.

Step 2. Skip single crochet just made, insert hook in next chain stitch, yarn over and pull loop through the chain stitch and the loop on the hook at same time.

The first slip stitch is done and a new loop is on the hook.

Make a slip stitich in each chain stitch across Strap to other Side, slip stitch in first single crochet stitch on side edge. Fasten off.

Lesson 7
Granny Square Hot Pad

In this pattern, you will learn to work in joined rounds, right side and wrong side of work, and learn to sew crochet pieces together.

You will be making a chain (ch) stitch from Lesson 2, a double crochet (dc) from Lesson 5 and a slip stitch from Lesson 6.

Materials

- Medium (worsted) weight yarn:
  - 1 oz/50 yds/28g solid color for round 1
  - 1 oz/50 yds/28g multicolored for round 2
  - 2 oz/100 yds/56g solid color for round 3
- Size G/6/4mm crochet hook
- Tapestry needle

Hot Pad

SQUARE
Make 8.
Round 1: Using the solid-color yarn for round 1, make 4 chains.

Slip stitch in the first chain made to form a crochet ring *(see photo 1)*.

Make 3 chains, make 2 double crochet stitches in the ring by inserting the hook through the center of the ring as you make the stitches.

Make 2 chains, [make 3 double crochet in the ring, make 2 chains] 3 times.

To join the beginning and the end of the round together, make a slip stitch in third chain of beg chain-3 *(see photo 2)*; hook yarn and draw it through the chain and through the loop on the hook; you have now joined the round. Fasten off.

RIGHT & WRONG SIDE OF WORK
When working in rounds, the right side (RS) of your stitches is always facing you.

If you turn your work over, then you have the back side of your stitches and the wrong side (WS) of your work.

Round 2: With right side (RS) of your work facing, using the multicolored yarn for round 2, join with a slip stitch in any of the chain spaces on last round.

To Join With a Slip Stitch

Step 1. Make a slip knot and put it on the hook.

Step 2. Insert the hook in the chain space, yarn over and pull the loop through the chain space and the loop on the hook.

Make 3 chains, make 2 double crochet in the same chain space, make 2 chains, make 3 more double crochet in the same chain space.

*Make 2 chains, skip the next 3 stitches on the last round, make (3 double crochet, 2 chains and 3 more double crochet) in the next chain space, repeat from the * 2 more times.

Make 2 chains, join with a slip stitch in the top 3rd chain of beginning chain-3. Fasten off (see photo 3).

Round 3: With right side of your work facing you, using the solid-color yarn for round 3, join with a slip stitch in the first chain space on last round.

Make 3 chains, make 2 more double crochet in the first chain space.

Make 2 chains, make 3 more double crochet stitches in the first chain space.

[Make 1 chain, skip the next 3 stitches on the last round, make 3 double crochet in the next chain space, make 1 chain, skip the next 3 stitches on the last round, make (3 double crochet, 2 chains and 3 more double crochet) in the next chain space] 3 times.

Make 1 chain, skip the next 3 stitches on the last round, make 3 double crochet in the next chain space, make 1 chain, skip the next 3 stitches on the last round, join with a slip stitch in the top of the chain-3. Fasten off (see photo 4).

ASSEMBLY

Thread the tapestry needle with the solid-color yarn for round 3.

Match 1 edge on 2 Squares together.

Working through the back loop of the stitches on each edge (see illustration A),

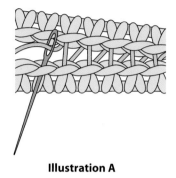

Illustration A

sew the squares together from corner to corner (see photo 5).

All the edges will be sewn together through the back loops.

Sew 4 Squares with right sides together (you will have the wrong side facing you, so your stitches will be on the back of your work) to make 1 large Square.

Hold both large Squares with wrong sides together, with 1 large Square on top of the other. Sew together all the way around the outside edge. ●

ican CROCHET

Lesson 8
Working With Two Strands Afghan

In this pattern, you will learn how to crochet with 2 strands of yarn held together at the same time.

You will be making a chain (ch) stitch from Lesson 2, a single crochet (sc) from Lesson 3 and a double crochet (dc) stitch from Lesson 5.

Materials
- Medium (worsted) weight yarn:
    28 oz/1,400 yds/794g
    multicolored yarn
    4 oz/200 yds/113g each
    purple and blue
- Size H/8/5.5mm crochet hook
- 3-inch square piece of carboard

Afghan

Row 1: With multicolored yarn, make 144 chains, make a double crochet in 4th chain from hook (the first 3 chains will count as your first double crochet) make a double crochet in each chain across, turn.

Row 2: Make 3 chains, these 3 chains will count as first double crochet, in each double crochet across, turn.

Row 3: Make 4 chains, these 4 chains will count as first double crochet and the first chain space, make a double crochet in next stitch *(see photo 1)*, [skip the next stitch on the last row, make a chain

1 and make a double crochet in next stitch] 70 times, and you will be working the last double crochet in the top of the turning chain at the end of the row.

Row 4: Make 3 chains, these 3 chains will count as first double crochet, double crochet in each double crochet and in each chain-1 space across, turn.

Row 5: Make 3 chains, these 3 chains will count as first double crochet, double crochet in each double crochet across, turn.

Row 6: Make 4 chains, these 4 chains will count as first double crochet and the first chain space, make a double crochet in next stitch, [skip the next stitch on the last row, make a chain 1 and make a double crochet in next stitch] 70 times, and you will be working the last double crochet in the top of the turning chain at the end of the row.

Rows 7–96: Rep rows 4, 5 and 6 consecutively over and over again until you have 96 rows or as long as you want. At end of last row, fasten off.

Remember you will have to have more yarn if you make it larger.

How to Make a Pompom

Cut 1 strand purple, lay across 1 edge of cardboard *(see photo 2)*.

Wrap purple yarn over and over again around cardboard approximately 150 times, covering strand. Fasten off.

Cut loops at 1 end as shown in photo 3.

Tie first strand tightly around all strands *(see photo 4)*.

Using ends of tie, attach 1 Pompom to each corner on Afghan.

To Work Chains to Weave Through Chain Spaces

Holding 2 strands of solid color together as 1, make 142 or more chains. Fasten off.

Take strands at 1 end and tie to the end of the first crochet of the row *(see photo 5)*.

Take free end and weave through spaces over and under double crochet stitches *(see photo 6)* all the way across to opposite end.

Tie rem end to last crochet stitch, pull out any extra chains and hide ends.

Make 16 blue and 15 purple Chains, (remember, if you have made yours longer, then you will need more Chains), weaving first 1 color then the next color all the way to top. ●

Lesson 9
Continuous Rounds Hat

In this pattern, you will learn to work in continuous rounds. You also will learn about increasing and about stitch counts. You will learn how to make a reverse single crochet (reverse sc) for a decorative edging.

You will be making a chain (ch) stitch from Lesson 2, a single crochet (sc) from Lesson 3 and a slip stitch from Lesson 6.

Finished Size
Hat will fit up to a 21-inch head.

Materials
- Medium (worsted) weight yarn:
    - 3 oz/150 yds/85g solid color
- Size G/6/4mm crochet hook
- Stitch markers

Pattern Notes
Continuous rounds in crochet are worked around and around without joining with a slip stitch as in joined rounds.

When working in continuous rounds that have increases or decreases, it is important to keep up with the first stitch of each round so you can make the right number of stitches.

To do this, you place a marker in the stitch when it is done.

Several things can be used to mark stitches, such as bobby pins, knit stitch markers and even a piece of yarn that is a different color.

When the first stitch of each new round is made, the marker is taken out of the last round and moved to the new round.

Sometimes you will want to leave the markers in place for several rounds at a time in case it is a lengthy or detailed pattern.

Hat
Round 1: With solid-color yarn, make 4 chains, make a slip stitch in the first chain of the chain-4 to form a crochet ring (see Lesson 7 photo 1).

Make a single crochet in the ring (see Lesson 3), place a marker in this stitch.

Make 7 more single crochet in the ring, do not join the first and last stitch of the rounds unless the instructions tell you to (see photo 1). (8 single crochet made)

In some crochet patterns it is important to have the correct number of stitches in each row or round.

The number inside a set of parentheses ( ) at the end of a row or round is called a stitch count.

This is a reminder to make sure you have the right amount of stitches so the next round you make will be right.

①

Round 2: Make 2 single crochet in the marked first stitch.

Whenever you make more than one stitch into a stitch, it is called an increase (inc). This is done to make a piece larger or to add shaping to a piece.

Make 2 single crochet in each stitch around *(see photo 2)*. *(16 single crochet made)*

Rounds 3 & 4: Make a single crochet in the first stitch and move the marker to the stitch just made.

Be sure to move the marker to the first stitch of each new round you make *(see photo 3)*.

Make 2 single crochet in the next stitch.

[Make a single crochet in the next stitch, make 2 single crochet in the next stitch] 7 times. *(24 single crochet made on round 3; 36 single crochet made on round 4)*

Round 5: Make a single crochet in each stitch around.

Round 6: [Make a single crochet in each of the next 3 stitches, make 2 single crochet in the next stitch] 8 times. *(45 single crochet)*

Round 7: Make a single crochet in each stitch around.

Round 8: Make a single crochet in the first stitch, [make a single crochet in each of the next 3 stitches, make 2 single crochet in the next stitch] 11 times. *(56 single crochet)*

Round 9: Make a single crochet in each stitch around.

Round 10: Make a single crochet in the first stitch, [make a single crochet in each of the next 4 stitches, make 2 single crochet in the next stitch] 11 times. *(67 single crochet)*

Rounds 11 & 12: Make a single crochet in each stitch around.

Round 13: Make a single crochet in the first stitch, [make a single crochet in each of the next 5 stitches, make 2 single crochet in the next stitch] 11 times. *(78 single crochet)*

Rounds 14–16: Make a single crochet in each stitch around.

Round 17: Make a single crochet in the first stitch, [make a single crochet in each of the next 6 stitches, make 2 single crochet in the next stitch] 11 times. *(89 single crochet)*

Rounds 18–35: Make a single crochet in each stitch around.

At the end of the last round, join with a slip stitch in the marked single crochet made for that round.

Round 36: Make 1 chain, working from left to right, reverse single crochet in each stitch around.

To Make Reverse Single Crochet

For regular crochet, you work in a right-to-left direction. For reverse single crochet, you work in the opposite direction, which gives this decorative edging stitch a twisted-rope look.

Step 1. Insert the hook through the stitch to the right of the turning chain 1 *(see photos 4 and 5)*, yarn over and pull through *(see photo 6)*. This loop should be loose enough to come up and cross over the turning chain.

Step 2. Yarn over again and pull through both loops on the hook *(see photo 7)*.

The first reverse single crochet is done and a new loop is on the hook *(see photo 8)*.

Step 3. For the next reverse single crochet, insert the hook through the next stitch to the right of the last reverse single crochet made *(see photo 8)*.

Step 4. Yarn over and pull through *(see photo 9)*, remember to pull this loop up so it is loose enough to cross over the front of the last stitch.

Step 5. Yarn over again and pull through both loops on the hook.

Continue repeating Steps 3–5 until you get back to the turning chain 1. Join with a slip stitch at the base of the first reverse single crochet made. Fasten off.

FINISHING
You can add additional decoration by making a Scrunchie *(see Lesson 3)* or Daisies *(see Lesson 10)*.

Sewing on large colorful buttons can create a different look for your hat.

Try making the last round of reverse single crochet in a different color. ●

i can CROCHET

Lesson 10
Treble Crochet Daisy Accent

In this pattern, you will learn to make a treble crochet (tr) stitch.

You will be working in joined rounds.

You will be making a chain (ch) from Lesson 2, a single crochet (sc) stitch from Lesson 3, a half double crochet (hdc) stitch from Lesson 4 and a slip stitch from Lesson 6.

Finished Sizes
About 3 inches across the middle of the small daisy.

About 4½ inches across the middle of the large daisy.

Materials For Each Small Daisy
• Medium (worsted) weight yarn:
    small amount (about 10 yards) white
    small amount (about 5 yards) yellow
• Size G/6/4mm crochet hook

Materials For Each Large Daisy
• Medium (worsted) weight yarn:
    small amount (about 20 yards) white
    small amount (about 10 yards) yellow
• Size H/8/5mm crochet hook

Small Daisy
Round 1: With size G hook and yellow yarn, make 4 chains, slip stitch in the first chain to form a crochet ring, make 3 chains *(this counts as the first half double crochet)*, make 15 half double crochet in the ring *(see photo 1)*.

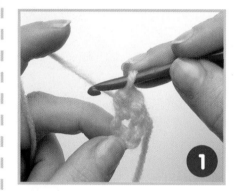

Join with a slip stitch *(see Lesson 7)* in the top of the chain-3 at the beginning of the round. Fasten off. *(16 half double crochet made)*

Round 2: Join the white yarn with a slip stitch in any stitch on the last round.

Now you are ready to make a petal. You will make all of the following stitches into the same stitch.

Make a single crochet in the next stitch, make 3 chains *(see photo 2),* insert the hook in the same stitch as the single crochet to make a treble crochet.

To Make a Treble Crochet Stitch

Step 1. Yarn over 2 times *(see photo 3)*, insert the hook in the stitch.

Step 2. Yarn over again and pull through *(see photo 4)*, you will have 4 loops on the hook.

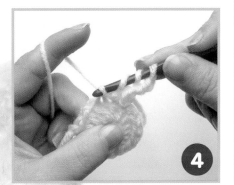

Step 3. [Yarn over and pull through 2 loops on the hook] 3 times *(see photos 5–7)*.

The treble crochet is done and a new loop is on the hook.

Make 3 chains, make a single crochet in the same stitch as the treble crochet; the first petal is done *(see photo 8)*.

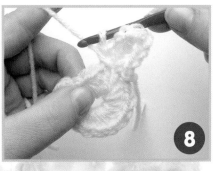

Step 4. Slip stitch in the next stitch.

Step 5. For the next petal, make (a single crochet, 3 chains, a treble crochet, 3 more chains and 1 more single crochet) in the next stitch; the 2nd petal is done *(see photo 9)*.

Repeat steps 4 and 5 to make 6 more petals.

Join with a slip stitch in the first slip stitch at the beginning of the round. Fasten off.

Large Daisy

Using size H hook and 2 strands of yarn held together as you work *(see Lesson 8)*, repeat the instructions for the Small Daisy.

The Small Daisy can be used to decorate picture frames, clothing, hats, belts and hair clips. You can even sew them on jeans as a decorative patch to cover a small tear or spot!

The Large Daisy can be used as a coaster, a wall decal, a binder decal, backpack patch or a package decoration instead of a bow.

These Daisies can be sewn or glued to almost anything you want to put them on. ●

STITCH GUIDE

FOR MORE COMPLETE INFORMATION, VISIT **ANNIESCATALOG.COM/STITCHGUIDE**

STITCH ABBREVIATIONS

beg	begin/begins/beginning
bpdc	back post double crochet
bpsc	back post single crochet
bptr	back post treble crochet
CC	contrasting color
ch(s)	chain(s)
ch-	refers to chain or space previously made (i.e., ch-1 space)
ch sp(s)	chain space(s)
cl(s)	cluster(s)
cm	centimeter(s)
dc	double crochet (singular/plural)
dc dec	double crochet 2 or more stitches together, as indicated
dec	decrease/decreases/decreasing
dtr	double treble crochet
ext	extended
fpdc	front post double crochet
fpsc	front post single crochet
fptr	front post treble crochet
g	gram(s)
hdc	half double crochet
hdc dec	half double crochet 2 or more stitches together, as indicated
inc	increase/increases/increasing
lp(s)	loop(s)
MC	main color
mm	millimeter(s)
oz	ounce(s)
pc	popcorn(s)
rem	remain/remains/remaining
rep(s)	repeat(s)
rnd(s)	round(s)
RS	right side
sc	single crochet (singular/plural)
sc dec	single crochet 2 or more stitches together, as indicated
sk	skip/skipped/skipping
sl st(s)	slip stitch(es)
sp(s)	space(s)/spaced
st(s)	stitch(es)
tog	together
tr	treble crochet
trtr	triple treble
WS	wrong side
yd(s)	yard(s)
yo	yarn over

YARN CONVERSION

OUNCES TO GRAMS		GRAMS TO OUNCES	
1	28.4	25	7/8
2	56.7	40	1 2/3
3	85.0	50	1 3/4
4	113.4	100	3 1/2

UNITED STATES		UNITED KINGDOM
sl st (slip stitch)	=	sc (single crochet)
sc (single crochet)	=	dc (double crochet)
hdc (half double crochet)	=	htr (half treble crochet)
dc (double crochet)	=	tr (treble crochet)
tr (treble crochet)	=	dtr (double treble crochet)
dtr (double treble crochet)	=	ttr (triple treble crochet)
skip	=	miss

Reverse single crochet (reverse sc): Ch 1, sk first st, working from left to right, insert hook in next st from front to back, draw up lp on hook, yo and draw through both lps on hook.

Chain (ch): Yo, pull through lp on hook.

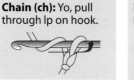

Single crochet (sc): Insert hook in st, yo, pull through st, yo, pull through both lps on hook.

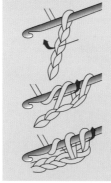

Double crochet (dc): Yo, insert hook in st, yo, pull through st, [yo, pull through 2 lps] twice.

Front loop (front lp) Back loop (back lp)

Front Loop Back Loop

Front post stitch (fp): Back post stitch (bp): When working post st, insert hook from right to left around post of st on previous row.

Back Front

← Post of Stitch

Half double crochet (hdc): Yo, insert hook in st, yo, pull through st, yo, pull through all 3 lps on hook.

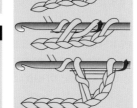

Double treble crochet (dtr): Yo 3 times, insert hook in st, yo, pull through st, [yo, pull through 2 lps] 4 times.

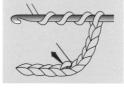

Slip stitch (sl st): Insert hook in st, pull through both lps on hook.

Chain color change (ch color change) Yo with new color, draw through last lp on hook.

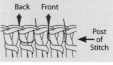

Double crochet color change (dc color change) Drop first color, yo with new color, draw through last 2 lps of st.

Treble crochet (tr): Yo twice, insert hook in st, yo, pull through st, [yo, pull through 2 lps] 3 times.

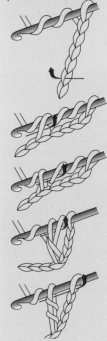

Single crochet decrease (sc dec): (Insert hook, yo, draw lp through) in each of the sts indicated, yo, draw through all lps on hook.

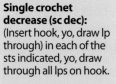
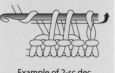

Example of 2-sc dec

Half double crochet decrease (hdc dec): (Yo, insert hook, yo, draw lp through) in each of the sts indicated, yo, draw through all lps on hook.

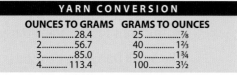

Example of 2-hdc dec

Double crochet decrease (dc dec): (Yo, insert hook, yo, draw lp through, yo, draw through 2 lps on hook) in each of the sts indicated, yo, draw through all lps on hook.

Example of 2-dc dec

Treble crochet decrease (tr dec): Holding back last lp of each st, tr in each of the sts indicated, yo, pull through all lps on hook.

Example of 2-tr dec

LEFT-HANDED STITCH GUIDE

STITCH ABBREVIATIONS

beg	begin/begins/beginning
bpdc	back post double crochet
bpsc	back post single crochet
bptr	back post treble crochet
CC	contrasting color
ch(s)	chain(s)
ch-	refers to chain or space previously made (i.e., ch-1 space)
ch sp(s)	chain space(s)
cl(s)	cluster(s)
cm	centimeter(s)
dc	double crochet (singular/plural)
dc dec	double crochet 2 or more stitches together, as indicated
dec	decrease/decreases/decreasing
dtr	double treble crochet
ext	extended
fpdc	front post double crochet
fpsc	front post single crochet
fptr	front post treble crochet
g	gram(s)
hdc	half double crochet
hdc dec	half double crochet 2 or more stitches together, as indicated
inc	increase/increases/increasing
lp(s)	loop(s)
MC	main color
mm	millimeter(s)
oz	ounce(s)
pc	popcorn
rem	remain/remains/remaining
rep(s)	repeat(s)
rnd(s)	round(s)
RS	right side
sc	single crochet (singular/plural)
sc dec	single crochet 2 or more stitches together, as indicated
sk	skip/skipped/skipping
sl st(s)	slip stitch(es)
sp(s)	space(s)/spaced
st(s)	stitch(es)
tog	together
tr	treble crochet
trtr	triple treble
WS	wrong side
yd(s)	yard(s)
yo	yarn over

YARN CONVERSION

OUNCES TO GRAMS		GRAMS TO OUNCES	
1	28.4	25	7/8
2	56.7	40	1 2/3
3	85.0	50	1 3/4
4	113.4	100	3 1/2

UNITED STATES		UNITED KINGDOM
sl st (slip stitch)	=	sc (single crochet)
sc (single crochet)	=	dc (double crochet)
hdc (half double crochet)	=	htr (half treble crochet)
dc (double crochet)	=	tr (treble crochet)
tr (treble crochet)	=	dtr (double treble crochet)
dtr (double treble crochet)	=	ttr (triple treble crochet)
skip	=	miss

Reverse single crochet (reverse sc): Ch 1, sk first st, working from right to left, insert hook in next st from front to back, draw up lp on hook, yo and draw through both lps on hook.

Chain (ch): Yo, pull through lp on hook.

Single crochet (sc): Insert hook in st, yo, pull through st, yo, pull through both lps on hook.

Double crochet (dc): Yo, insert hook in st, yo, pull through st, [yo, pull through 2 lps] twice.

Front loop (front lp) Back loop (back lp)

Back Loop   Front Loop

Front post stitch (fp): Back post stitch (bp): When working post st, insert hook from left to right around post of st on previous row.

Front   Back

← Post of Stitch

Half double crochet (hdc): Yo, insert hook in st, yo, pull through st, yo, pull through all 3 lps on hook.

Double treble crochet (dtr): Yo 3 times, insert hook in st, yo, pull through st, [yo, pull through 2 lps] 4 times.

Slip stitch (sl st): Insert hook in st, pull through both lps on hook.

Chain color change (ch color change) Yo with new color, draw through last lp on hook.

Double crochet color change (dc color change) Drop first color, yo with new color, draw through last 2 lps of st.

Treble crochet (tr): Yo twice, insert hook in st, yo, pull through st, [yo, pull through 2 lps] 3 times.

Single crochet decrease (sc dec): (Insert hook, yo, draw lp through) in each of the sts indicated, yo, draw through all lps on hook.

Example of 2-sc dec

Half double crochet decrease (hdc dec): (Yo, insert hook, yo, draw lp through) in each of the sts indicated, yo, draw through all lps on hook.

Example of 2-hdc dec

Double crochet decrease (dc dec): (Yo, insert hook, yo, draw lp through, yo, draw through 2 lps on hook) in each of the sts indicated, yo, draw through all lps on hook.

Example of 2-dc dec

Treble crochet decrease (tr dec): Holding back last lp of each st, tr in each of the sts indicated, yo, pull through all lps on hook.

Example of 2-tr dec

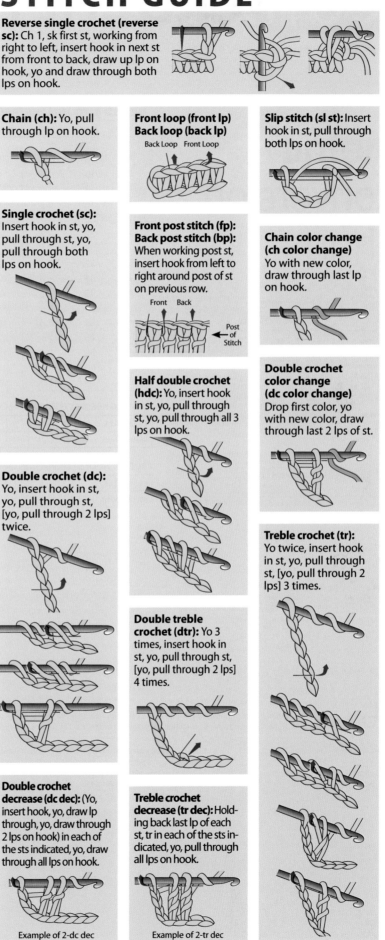

i can CROCHET

Metric Conversion Charts

METRIC CONVERSIONS

yards	x	.9144	=	metres (m)
yards	x	91.44	=	centimetres (cm)
inches	x	2.54	=	centimetres (cm)
inches	x	25.40	=	millimetres (mm)
inches	x	.0254	=	metres (m)

centimetres	x	.3937	=	inches
metres	x	1.0936	=	yards

INCHES INTO MILLIMETRES & CENTIMETRES (Rounded off slightly)

inches	mm	cm	inches	cm	inches	cm	inches	cm
1/8	3	0.3	5	12.5	21	53.5	38	96.5
1/4	6	0.6	5 1/2	14	22	56	39	99
3/8	10	1	6	15	23	58.5	40	101.5
1/2	13	1.3	7	18	24	61	41	104
5/8	15	1.5	8	20.5	25	63.5	42	106.5
3/4	20	2	9	23	26	66	43	109
7/8	22	2.2	10	25.5	27	68.5	44	112
1	25	2.5	11	28	28	71	45	114.5
1 1/4	32	3.2	12	30.5	29	73.5	46	117
1 1/2	38	3.8	13	33	30	76	47	119.5
1 3/4	45	4.5	14	35.5	31	79	48	122
2	50	5	15	38	32	81.5	49	124.5
2 1/2	65	6.5	16	40.5	33	84	50	127
3	75	7.5	17	43	34	86.5		
3 1/2	90	9	18	46	35	89		
4	100	10	19	48.5	36	91.5		
4 1/2	115	11.5	20	51	37	94		

KNITTING NEEDLES CONVERSION CHART

Canada/U.S.	0	1	2	3	4	5	6	7	8	9	10	10½	11	13	15
Metric (mm)	2	2¼	2¾	3¼	3½	3¾	4	4½	5	5½	6	6½	8	9	10

CROCHET HOOKS CONVERSION CHART

Canada/U.S.	1/B	2/C	3/D	4/E	5/F	6/G	8/H	9/I	10/J	10½/K	N
Metric (mm)	2.25	2.75	3.25	3.5	3.75	4.25	5	5.5	6	6.5	9.0

Annie's® *I Can Crochet* is published by Annie's, 306 East Parr Road, Berne, IN 46711. Printed in USA. Copyright © 2012, 2017 Annie's. All rights reserved. This publication may not be reproduced in part or in whole without written permission from the publisher.

RETAIL STORES: If you would like to carry this publication or any other Annie's publications, visit AnniesWSL.com.

Every effort has been made to ensure that the instructions in this pattern book are complete and accurate. We cannot, however, take responsibility for human error, typographical mistakes or variations in individual work. Please visit AnniesCustomerService.com to check for pattern updates.

ISBN: 978-1-59635-641-2

10 11 12 13 14 15 16